BODY MODIFICATION

ANNE SCHRAFF

Artesian Press

P.O. Box 355, Buena Park, CA 90621

www.artesianpress.com

Nonfiction
eXtreme Customs Series

Body Modification	**1-58659-211-4**
Audio Cassette	**1-58659-127-4**
Audio CD	**1-58659-361-7**
Burials	1-58659-212-2
Audio Cassette	1-58659-128-2
Audio CD	1-58659-362-5
Fashion	1-58659-213-0
Audio Cassette	1-58659-129-0
Audio CD	1-58659-363-3
Food	1-58659-214-9
Audio Cassette	1-58659-130-4
Audio CD	1-58659-364-1
Tattoos	1-58659-210-6
Audio Cassette	1-58659-126-6
Audio CD	1-58659-360-9

Cover Photo by Eliot Elisofon, National Museum of African Art, Smithsonian Institution
Editor: Zac Miller
Project Coordinator: Cynthia Seville
Graphic Design: Tony Amaro
Photo Research: Donna Braunstein
©2006 Artesian Press

www.artesianpress.com

 Artesian **Press**

ISBN 1-58659-211-4

Contents

Word List

Aborigines (a-buh-RIG-en-eez) The indigenous people of a region. This usually refers to the natives of Australia.

AIDS (aidz) A disease caused by the HIV virus that makes it hard for the body to fight infection. AIDS stands for Acquired Immunodeficiency Syndrome.

archeologists (ark-ee-OL-uh-gists) These are scientists that study fossils, monuments, and things left behind by people who lived long ago.

autoclave (AW-toe-clave) An instrument that uses high heat and pressure to kill all the germs on such things as medical tools.

Benin (beh-NEEN) A small country in coastal west Africa.

Burmese (ber-MEEZ) A person or thing from Burma, a country also called Myanmar (MIE-un-mar), in Southeast Asia near China and India.

counterculture (COWN-ter-cul-tyer) A group of people whose beliefs and customs are different from the rest of society or the people of their community.

fraternities (frah-TER-nih-teez) Clubs with special rules for boys. They are usually found at colleges.

hepatitis (hep-uh-TIE-tus) A serious disease that affects the body's liver.

HIV virus (H-I-V VIE-rus) A group of tiny living things that kill cells of the body's immune systems so the body can't fight off diseases and infection. It can cause AIDS.

Luba (LOO-bah) A group or tribe of people who live in Zaire, central Africa.

mainstream society (MANE-streem seh-SIE-eh-tee) People who follow the "normal" customs and rules of their culture.

Makonde (mah-KON-day) Groups or tribes of people who live in Tanzania (tan-zuh-NEE-uh) and Mozambique (moe-zam-BEEK), countries in southeast Africa.

Maori (MOW-uh-ree) People native to New Zealand.

Padong (pa-DONG) A group or tribe of people who live in the hills of Thailand (TIE-land), a country in Southeast Asia.

red ochre (red OH-ker) A kind of paint made from iron ore.

ritual (RICH-yew-uhl) A social custom or ceremony that is repeated, has a certain form, and follows the same rules, like a wedding, for example.

Scarification (skar-ih-fih-KAY-shun) The use of scars to make permanent marks and designs on the skin.

self-esteem (self eh-STEEM) Feeling confident, or good about yourself.

sororities (seh-ROR-eh-teez) Clubs with special rules for girls. They are usually found at colleges.

staph (staff) Short for staphylococcus (staff-eh-loe-COH-kus), a kind of bacteria that can infect your skin and mucus membranes, and make you sick.

steroids (STIR-roydz) Dangerous drugs sometimes used to build up muscles to an abnormal size.

strep (strep) Short for streptococcus (strep-teh-COH-kus), a kind of bacteria that can cause illness. It often affects the throat.

Sudan (soo-DAN) A country in north central Africa south of Egypt.

syphilis (SIFF-uh-lis) A contagious, sexually transmitted disease that can cause rashes, sores, brain damage, and death if not treated.

Tonga (TAHN-geh) An island country in the southwest Pacific Ocean.

tuberculosis (too-ber-kyew-LOE-sis) A communicable disease that usually affects the lungs. It is often called TB.

Zapotec (zah-peh-TEK) American Indians who live in Mexico.

Chapter 1

Anything for Beauty and Status

These Padong women are wearing brass coils.

Curious tourists crowded into the Tha Ton camp in Thailand to see the colorfully dressed Burmese (ber-MEEZ) women known simply as the "Giraffe Women." There the tourists saw thirty-two women whose necks appeared to have been "stretched." How? The women had worn brass coils around their necks since they were young girls.

When the girls were about ten years old, heavy brass coils were fitted around their necks. Some of these coils weighed as much as 11 pounds. That's more than two sacks of potatoes! As the girls grew, the coils were removed and replaced with longer, heavier ones. These coils gradually forced the ribs downward, making it look as though the neck was getting longer. The necks of Giraffe Women appeared to be twice as long as our own.

According to a Burmese custom, only Padong (pa-DONG) girls born on a Wednesday under a full moon had their necks stretched. At first, the coils were a bit uncomfortable. Soon the girls became used to them. Some people claimed that if the coils were removed, the girls' necks would collapse because they had been weakened by the weight of the coils. Others said that was not true. They believed that the girls and women could remove the coils for cleaning, and that their necks would not collapse. They argued that if a Giraffe Woman removed her coil, her shoulder muscles would slowly move back up to their normal position.

No one really knows how or why this strange custom of wearing neck coils started in Burma. Some people say that the coils around the neck protected women from tigers, which often leaped for the throat. Others say the coils showed that a person was rich or was very important in the community. One Burmese legend even says that the Padong people of Burma were the descendents of a long-necked dragon, and neck lengthening was done to honor this belief.

Every year, about 10,000 people pay money to visit the camp where they can see the Giraffe Women. One of these women earns a small income each month by letting the tourists come

13

to see her. She is happy to earn money this way because before she came to Thailand, she worked in the rice fields of Burma and was paid a lot less.

Neck "stretching" is a form of body modification, which means that people change the way that their bodies look. Some do it to appear more beautiful. Others do it just to fit in with their society, to continue a tradition, custom, or ritual (RICH-yew-uhl), or to gain status, which makes them feel more important. All kinds of people all over the world practice some form of body modification. Neck stretching may seem weird or even dangerous to people who live in what we call the "civilized world," but we can find many forms of body modification right in our own society.

Some people choose to make their muscles larger than normal through exercising many hours every day. Others try to get the same results by taking drugs, which can be very dangerous. Some women believe they need to be very slim or even skinny to be beautiful, and so they starve themselves. They often get so thin that they become very ill and must go to the hospital for treatment. Other women may wish for larger breasts. Many men and women want smaller noses. They are often willing to have surgery to get them. People all over the world keep trying to improve or change the bodies they were born with. It is easy to say that the body-altering customs of other cultures or societies are strange or don't make sense while ignoring the strange things some of us do to our bodies.

Chapter 2

How to Get Ahead

The oldest form of body modification is head shaping. The custom of changing the shape of heads goes all the way back to the beginning of human history. The oldest example of this form of body modification can be seen in the cave dwelling ancestors of modern man, who lived 40,000 to 150,000 years ago. Scientists have found skulls with flattened frontal bones. Skulls of both males and females that were found in a cave in northeast China show that the frontal bone had been flattened. A skull found in Australia in 1925 had a very long and flattened frontal bone. It is certain that both the Chinese and Australian skulls were flattened on purpose by people and were not shaped that way naturally.

Even these early people wanted to change the way they looked. They may have wanted to appear more beautiful, or they may have wanted to show that they were important people or that they belonged to a certain group in their society.

Cave dwellers didn't have fancy homes, expensive cars, or the latest technological gadgets to make them feel important or better than their neighbors. They used body modification and decoration to show the others in their community that they were important. These people could not show off expensive jewelry or a TV satellite dish, but they could brag about having flatter skulls than their neighbors.

Other early people also practiced head shaping. The ancient people of South America and Mexico believed that the shape of a person's head showed whether he or she had been born into a royal family. Because infants and

A Mayan ceramic vase showing a person of royalty with a reshaped head.

children have softer bones, their parents used pads, boards, and strips of cloth to shape the young heads the way they wanted them to look.

The Maya people, for example, put wooden forms on their babies' foreheads to reshape the face. This form made a long slope that started at the bridge of the nose and angled back to the top of the head. The people thought that these sloping foreheads were beautiful.

Some Greeks, Romans, and North American native peoples also tightly wrapped babies' heads to make a shape that they thought was beautiful. They bound headboards to the back of the babies' heads to make their skulls longer. The people thought this made their children smarter and more handsome.

Rather than flattening their heads, some people in modern New Guinea flattened their noses. They put shells, animal tusks, and feathers in their noses to flatten them out. Some Polynesian people even broke their noses just to make their profiles flatter.

Chapter 3

Ear Piercing and Stretching

This ear is decorated with multiple piercings and a spacer which is used to strech out a piercing.

One of the most well-known forms of changing a person's appearance is piercing. Perhaps the most common and popular type of piercing is making holes in earlobes for earrings. Earrings date back thousands of years to western Asia. It wasn't unusual for those ancient people to pierce their earlobes. Two of the most popular kinds of earrings were hoops and pendants. The earliest earrings discovered by archeologists (ark-ee-OL-uh-gists) date back about 4,500 years ago. They were discovered at the royal graves of Ur in Iraq.

To make a hole in the earlobes, people used metal, bone, or tools made from shells to pierce the flesh. Many cultures thought of piercing as a sign of growing up. For others, it had a religious meaning. For some of the early Native Americans in southeast Alaska, ear piercing showed a person's rank or position in society. In the big community feasts they pierced the rims of children's ears. Each time they held another feast, more holes were made in the children's ears. The children of people who were very important in the community had more piercings than the children of less important people.

Hoop earrings made from gold, silver, and bronze were uncovered in ancient graves in Crete, near Greece, and are about 4,000 years old. During the time of the New Kingdom in Egypt, about 3,000 years ago, earplugs became popular. To wear earplugs, the earlobe hole had to be stretched wider so the plug would fit. Earplugs can be seen on some famous statues from that time.

In Greece, pendant or hanging earrings were popular. Usually, they were shaped like a peacock, dove, or swan. Women from rich families in Rome wore earrings that had gemstones, such as sapphires, emeralds, topazes, and aquamarines.

By the middle of the seventeenth century in Europe, well-dressed women felt it was necessary to have their ears pierced. Very large earrings, often made from gold and silver, became fashionable. These earrings were so heavy that it often hurt to wear them. Some women put ribbons through the earrings and then wrapped the ribbons around the tops of their ears or tied them to their hair. This took some of the pressure off

Queen Victoria with large earrings

their earlobes. Still, women who wore the extremely heavy earrings, which had many gemstones, found that their earlobes stretched, even though they didn't want them to. England's Queen Victoria liked to wear large earrings. After forcing her earlobes to support the weight of these monster-sized pieces of jewelry most of her life, her earlobes were obviously stretched. Her drooping earlobes are plainly seen in portraits that were painted when she was older.

In the 1860s, long earrings that hung down almost to the shoulder were popular. Some tried to be different and to get people to look at them by using fish swimming in bowls, landscapes, or small arrows made to look like they had been shot through the earlobe. Brazilian beetles, with their brilliant green shells, were used to make earrings. Some kinds of earrings were made of hardened lava from volcanoes.

Stretching earlobes was a common practice in Africa. The women of one tribe wore huge wooden discs in their ears. These women had to wrap their long earlobes around their ears so they wouldn't have loops of skin dangling in their faces.

There are many examples of stretched earlobes in Asia, too. Young girls wear heavier and heavier jewelry, which causes their earlobes to stretch. This custom continues on the island of

Borneo, a part of Malaysia. In Africa, the custom is no longer very popular, but tourists still see many older people with tattered and torn earlobes, caused by stretching.

Chapter 4

Piercing in Other Places

Although ear piercing and the custom of wearing earrings has been a part of human history for many centuries, other types of body piercing were more popular in Africa, India, Indonesia, and North and South America. Earlobes and the harder part of the ear were pierced to show a person's passage through different stages of life. Nostrils and lips were also pierced.

Piercing causes bleeding. In many cultures, the blood that came from piercing was important. It was often thought of as an offering to the gods or to ancestors.

In Alaska, men and women would commonly pierce their lips. They then wore lip plugs. Men wore either one lip plug in the center

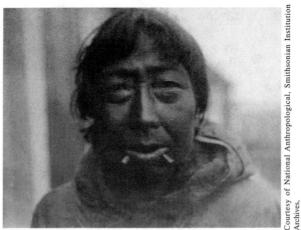

Man with lip plugs, King Island, Alaska

of his mouth or he wore two, one on each side of his mouth. A man wearing two lip plugs looked a bit like a walrus. Young men had plugs fitted into their lips to show that they had reached adulthood. Women wore one center lip plug.

Men and women made the holes in their lips larger by slowly stretching them. Sometimes the holes got so large that the whole lip was pulled down so that the teeth and gums could always be seen. Very large plugs made it difficult to speak or even eat, so they had to be removed during conversations and meals.

As jewelry and other body decorations became larger, it became necessary to make the pierced holes larger, too. People in Peru put big carvings of golden eagles in the side of their noses. Nose rings were worn on either side of the nose or right in the middle through the wall between the nostrils. Nose piercing was popular in Mexico and is still done all over India and Pakistan. Yo-yo-sized hollow cylinders made of a hard stone used to be put into the widened earlobes of the Zapotec (zah-peh-TEK) people of Mexico. Many people believed that putting these large objects in their ears, nose, and lips made them more important in society.

Some ancient people pierced their tongues, a practice that has become more popular today. The Maya people of Central America pierced their tongues because they thought it was a way to communicate with the spirits of their ancestors during ceremonies.

Scarring or scarification (skar-ih-fih-KAY-shun) of the tongue was also done. Some Aborigines (a-buh-RIG-en-eez) of Australia cut and then burned their tongues to show their pain when someone died. Even though the tongue is extremely sensitive and bleeds a lot when pierced or cut, tongue piercing is increasing in popularity as a fashion statement.

Most body parts have been pierced at one time or another in one culture or another. Regardless of the part being pierced or the people doing it, the reasons remain the same: beauty and status.

Chapter 5

Scarification

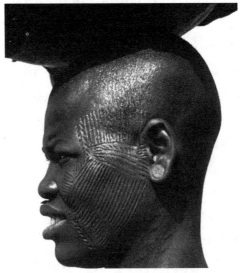

Photograph by Eliot Elisofon, 1959 Image no. 2635, Eliot Elisofon Photographic Archives, National Museum of African Art, Smithsonian Institution

Woman with facial scarification carrying basket

One of the most painful forms of body modification is using scars to make marks on the skin. This is called scarification. The skin is cut on purpose to leave permanent patterns of scars.

This process is a bit like tattooing with one big difference: the end result must be scars that are raised on the skin in the form of raised lines or beadsized bumps. Because tattoos don't show as well on darker skin, scarification is often used instead. Most people in our culture try their best to avoid scars from burns, cuts, and accidents. However, people who perform scarification think that smooth skin is ugly. Those who practice scarification not only make cuts in the skin, they also try to slow the healing to make even bigger scars.

In scarification, deep cuts are made on the face and body, using either primitive or modern instruments. Then things like clay or ashes are rubbed into the wounds to slow down the healing. Some scarification methods are terribly painful. First the skin is cut, then ground charcoal, ashes, or castor oil and red ochre (red OH-ker), a kind of paint made from iron ore, are rubbed into the wounds to make them darker and more visible. The scars are then re-cut and colored again, making them even more dramatic. The goal is to have permanent bumps on the skin. Scarification is extremely painful, so in some cultures people willing to have it done to their bodies are respected as people of great courage.

Sometimes, scarification is done by burning or branding the skin. This leaves a raised scar. In the past, in parts of Europe and even in the United States, slaves and convicts were branded to make it more difficult for them to hide among free people if they escaped.

Most scarification has taken place in Africa. Ways of thinking have changed over the last 100 years, and scarification has been discouraged. But feelings are hard to change, and some people still think that patterns and designs of scars are more beautiful than smooth skin. Some people feel that the bonds

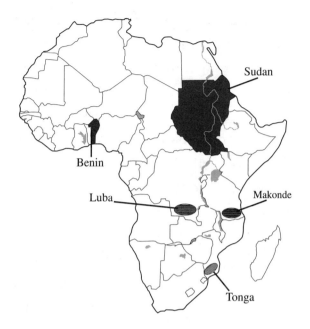

A map of Africa showing countries and tribal areas where scarification is performed.

of shared experiences of pain and courage make scarification an honored even valuable thing, somewhat like our attitudes towards hazing in sororities (seh-ROR-eh-teez) and fraternities (frah-TER-nih-teez). Scarification is regaining popularity in some places.

The type or style of scarification shows tribal identity. A double line of bumplike scars across the forehead shows a girl is from Tonga (TAHN-geh). Sometimes geometric shapes are cut, sometimes flowers, or even pictures. Six cuts in the forehead mark a boy as being from Sudan (soo-DAN). Girls in Benin (beh-NEEN) have four marks cut above their eyebrows near each eye. Benin boys carry three marks that are blade shaped and run from their throats to their stomachs. Zigzag lines or upside down V's on the chin, lips, cheeks, and nose advertise a person is from the Makonde (mah-KON-day) tribe. Among the Luba (LOO-bah) women of central Africa, scarification is used to enhance their bodies and make statements about their personal history.

Scarification is performed by a man or woman who has learned the skill from other masters. The method is very painful and bloody. The boy or girl to be scarified on the face is told to lie down on his or her back. Then patterns are

Sudanese woman with facial scars

cut into the face with a sharp knife. The wounds are then rubbed with charcoal, and the youth must sit in the sun until the charcoal dries. Several days go by before the face can be washed and the permanent dark lines can be seen. The procedure can be repeated three more times, every six months, to make the marks stand out more. The scars must rise from the skin like a ridge. Once the scarification is completed, the young person has proved to the adults that he or she is now ready to accept the duties of being a grown-up. Some believed that if a girl had the courage to undergo scarification she would show courage in the future when she gave birth to her own child. In some cultures, young people cannot get married unless they had been scarified. Growing up in our country today can sometimes be hard, but it is rarely so physically painful as it is for those youths who undergo scarification.

Some forms of body modification are done to the teeth. In some cultures, certain teeth were pulled, or they were filed to sharp points, dyed different colors, and fitted with gemstones or repositioned in the mouth. In some cultures, this is often done just before marriage. In our culture, a great deal of time and money is spent on making teeth look healthy, straight, and white, even when it involves considerable pain.

Philippine woman with filed teeth

A form of body modification that many people argue about is when a person of one particular race changes a physical feature to make himself or herself appear to be of a different or what he or she thinks is a better race. Lighter-skinned people might dye their skin a darker shade. Many light-skinned people lie out in the sun or go to tanning salons to make their skin darker. This can damage their skin over

37

time, but they do it because they think it makes them more attractive. Darker skinned people sometimes try to lighten their skin or straighten their hair in order to look as though they belong to a lighter-skinned race. Asian people often have a fold of skin on their upper eyelid, which makes their eyes appear narrow or slanted. Some Asian women have had surgery to remove this fold, making their eyes more rounded, more like the eyes of people from Europe.

This kind of modification is very different from using cosmetic surgery to correct a real deformity. However, a great deal of body modification is done every day with the only purpose being to change a feature that some people think is unattractive. People sometimes let themselves be influenced by what society or other people say is beautiful. Rather than being satisfied with their own individual features, they have surgery to make themselves look like other people's idea of what is attractive.

A very unusual effort to change the appearance of children took place in the Maya culture of Central America. Parents hung balls between the eyes of their young children to make them cross-eyed. They thought that being cross-eyed was a sign of great beauty.

Chapter 6

Foot Binding

Chinese woman with bound feet

One of the most widespread and often crippling forms of body modification in history was the practice of foot binding in China. Beginning about 1,000 years ago, young Chinese girls between the ages of two and eight had their feet tightly bound with cloth to keep them from growing. This practice went on for about 1,000 years. The government began to discourage it in 1912. Still, girls' feet were being bound up until 1949 when the government banned it and destroyed all the books that described foot binding. During all these years, millions of Chinese women had their feet bound.

The custom of foot binding began during the latter Tang Dynasty, when it was said that big feet on a woman were ugly and that a beautiful woman's feet should look like the "three-inch golden lotus," a beautiful flower. At first, only court dancers could have their feet bound. Then the custom spread to all the women in the royal court, and finally to the people of the countryside. A mother made the decision whether or not to bind her daughter's feet.

When the Mongols took over China

about 800 years ago, they kept the practice of foot binding because they believed it made women more helpless and weak. When small feet on women became expected in the Chinese culture, mothers who wanted their daughters to have good lives had no choice but to bind their daughters' feet. If women wanted to marry, they had to have small feet. An unmarried woman in China had a poor life. With no husband to support her, a single woman had nothing good to look forward to in life. Even after she died, with no husband or children to tend her grave, people believed that she wandered throughout eternity as a hungry ghost.

Foot binding usually began when a girl was between two and three years old. As an adult, her foot could not be longer than 3.9 inches, so it was necessary to adjust the bindings frequently. Bandages were tightly wound around the little girl's feet, and

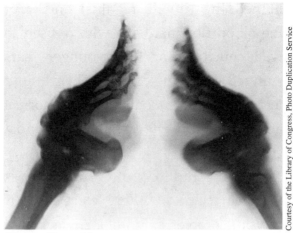

X-ray of bound feet

they were pulled tighter on a regular basis. The mother usually did this, but as the girl got older, she sometimes tightened her own bandages. Little girls learned at a young age that to have big feet as an adult was a horrible thing, so they gladly let their feet be bound.

The first two years of foot binding were the most painful. After that, the amount of pain was different for each girl. The girls were told to walk on their bound feet every day, even though it was not at all comfortable. Walking

43

helped the tiny feet adjust and kept the blood flowing. Girls who refused to walk much during their younger years suffered a lifetime of pain. Their bound feet were always too sensitive for normal activities, and the girls were almost crippled.

For the millions of women whose feet were bound, there were serious physical problems. Binding permanently disfigured the foot. Some women had pain all their lives. However, the majority of women were able to perform their daily chores quite well on their tiny feet.

As women with bound feet got older, they had a greater chance of falling and had more trouble getting out of a chair without help. Interviews with very old Chinese women in the 1990s showed that the women were not angry about having their feet bound. They accepted the foot binding as a custom of their culture and believed that their mothers had done what they thought was best for them. One woman bragged that she walked 10 miles to the rice fields every day on her bound feet and outworked any man.

During the many centuries when bound feet were customary, people could buy 3-inch shoes in many Chinese cities, and a number of factories mass-produced them. Even in 1991, when one factory began to produce the tiny shoes for elderly women who still needed them, they sold two thousand pairs every year. Now the factory is closed. Most of the women with bound feet have died. There has been no reported instance of foot binding in China for more than fifty years. If anyone tried to do it, he or she would be severely punished.

Chapter 7

Surgery and Chemicals

Moji Oluwa, bodybuilder and weight lifter, USA

As strange and cruel as foot binding seems to be, it is just one more example of the pain and suffering people will endure to reach a culture's idea of beauty or status.

Some men believe their bodies don't

have large enough muscles. They will spend most of their free time exercising to build up their muscles. That's not enough for some men. They want even bigger muscles than are natural. These men, and some women, too, inject themselves with steroids (STIR-oydz). Steroid drugs can make muscles grow bigger, but they can be very dangerous over time and can cause heart disease, behavior problems, and other health problems. Many girls don't like the overmuscled look, but body builders seem to do it for themselves, for their own idea of beauty.

Many women in modern times have been led to believe that large breasts make them more attractive. Some women who do not naturally have large breasts have turned to breast enlargement—yet another form of body modification.

When a healthy woman has surgery to make her breasts larger to improve her appearance, that is body modification

47

—changing one's appearance for reasons of beauty. Having breast surgery to restore or repair the body after medical treatments for illness does not fit into the category of body modification.

To many people, the idea of implanting a bag of chemicals into the body sounds bizarre and even frightening. Yet many women do it and feel that the risks they take are well worth their new sense of self-esteem (self eh-STEEM). Like the scarred young woman in Africa who treasures the bumps on her body as beauty marks and feels it is well worth the suffering she endures to get them, the woman who chooses breast enlargement feels the pain and risks of surgery are worth the results.

If a person believes a custom or practice is strange, cruel, or even wrong, it is often because of what he or she is used to. As the old saying goes, "Beauty is in the eye of the beholder." What is ugly to one person may be considered beautiful to another. Sometimes the idea of beauty is very personal, and it doesn't seem to matter what other people think. The body builder's girlfriend may not like the big-muscle look. A man married to a woman who wants breast enlargement may not like women with big breasts. People sometimes just get an idea in their heads of what they want to look like and don't care if other people disagree with their idea of beauty.

A photographer covered a large wall at the American Museum of Natural History in New York City with photographs of young American men and women who followed the body modification folk practices of the Maori (MOW-uh-ree) people of New Zealand. The young people, mostly from New York and San Francisco, sometimes lived among primitive tribes to get a better understanding of such traditions

Photograph by Nga Azarian, Courtesy of Graphic Muscle.

Maori man with facial scars

as body piercing and stretching earlobes. All of these young people then imitated these folk practices on their own bodies. Ear extension was very popular. But when some of the young Americans tried scarification, they found that it did not work as well on white skin as on darker skin. Still, the photographs show the amazing transformation of young white Americans into people who look like Maori warriors from New Zealand.

In recent years, body piercing has become popular, especially among young people. Earrings have been worn by all kinds of people in all kinds of cultures for centuries, but now it is not unusual to see ordinary people wearing nose rings. Celebrities often lead the way when something new and different becomes popular, and body piercing is no exception. Many popular singers and sports stars have their tongues, noses, nostrils, and lips pierced and decorated with jewelry. Often young people try to look like their favorite celebrity by doing the same thing.

Chapter 8

Strange Customs Today

Today, common jewelry used in body piercing includes the bead rings that screw into pierced eyebrows and the nostrils. Some people now have their earlobes pierced and then stretch the holes to fit larger pieces of jewelry. Sometimes the ear is pierced with as many as six or more holes so the person can wear several pieces of jewelry at the same time. Both the lobes and the hard part of the ear are pierced.

Before the 1970s, it was unusual to see earrings on a man. Now it has become very common. Again, many sports stars wear earrings, as do TV and movie stars.

Sometimes the bridge of the nose between the eyes is pierced and jewelry is worn there. It is difficult for the injury

Person with multiple facial piercings

www.punchstock.com

to heal at that spot. Cheek piercings some times result in damaged blood vessels and nerves.

There are many forms of facial piercing. Some eyebrow piercings join the brow line. If the area below the lip and above the chin is pierced, it requires a special attachment. Mouth piercings include the area around the lips and on the tongue. This area tends to swell up after piercing. When the tongue is pierced, it sometimes affects the way a person talks. At times, a person with a pierced tongue sounds like he or she has a lisp. Some people have described the speech of a person with a pierced tongue as sounding like marbles are being swished around inside the mouth.

As with tattoos, there are risks in body piercing. Anytime the body is pierced or pricked with a needle or other instrument, it is necessary to be extremely careful. All the instruments used, and the room where the piercing is done, should be completely clean and absolutely free of germs. This is accomplished by cleaning all the instruments using a special machine called an autoclave (AW-toe-clave), which destroys bacteria. Dirty instruments or surroundings can result in hepatitis (hep-uh-TIE-tus), syphilis (SIFF-uh-lis), tuberculosis (too-ber-kyew-LOE-sis), staph (staff) and strep infections, or even the HIV virus (H-I-V- VIE-rus), which leads to AIDS. In addition, a person who performs body piercing must be chosen carefully. He or she should be a well-trained professional.

The body naturally rejects foreign objects inserted into skin or tissue. Unless the piercing is done by a well-trained professional, serious problems can result.

There is a greater risk of catching a disease through body piercing than through tattooing, but risk exists anytime the skin is broken. Body piercing goes much deeper into the flesh, carrying the possibility of infection to more serious levels. Another problem results when the pierced area is not well cared for. Touching it before it heals can cause infection.

The area of the body that has been pierced remains inflamed and sore for a while. This is normal. But such symptoms as throbbing pain, a lot of redness, or an unusual oozing or discharge need immediate medical attention.

The modern-day way of piercing the body and creating a hole in the flesh for a piece of jewelry begins by cleaning the area to be pierced. The piercing itself is done with single-use hollow needles that are about two to three inches long.

Usually there are no painkillers used during a body piercing. Painkillers have their own risks, and they are not used unless absolutely necessary. There is pain during the piercing procedure, but it is usually not great enough to require painkillers.

Healing after a piercing depends on where the hole is. For earlobe piercing, the complete healing process takes about six weeks. When the hard part of the ear is pierced, two months are needed for healing. The tongue might take four to six weeks, while a cheek piercing may not heal for as long as four months.

Unlike tattoos, which are difficult to remove—especially if they are large and dark and located on an exposed area of the body, small holes drilled into the body disappear from view once jewelry is removed. Earlobe piercings sometimes close. But once a hole is drilled into the nose, lips, or tongue, some sign of it will probably remain.

Chapter 9

Why We Do It

Body modification is changing the natural appearance of the body in some way to make it look different. It can be something as simple as a young man with very little muscle tone deciding to exercise and lift weights until he has large muscles. Or it can be as complicated as a man who builds up his body with the help of dangerous drugs until he hardly looks like the person he used to be. Body modification can be a young woman who decides to eat healthy foods and start exercising so she has a slimmer figure. Or it can be a girl with a bad self-image who diets until she is dangerously thin, trying to look like a magazine model. There are health risks in such extreme behavior. Trying to get unusual or unnatural body measurements can be deadly.

History is filled with examples of body modification plans gone wrong, from removing ribs to get a thinner, more fashionable waist, to removing little toes in order to fit into smaller shoes. At one time, women made their waists appear much smaller by wearing a piece of clothing called a corset, which wrapped around their middle and was then tied very tightly. Sometimes these tight corsets, which tortured the wearers, actually damaged internal organs. They often caused the women to faint.

While piercings and other body modifications are done in such places as Africa and Polynesia to celebrate a new stage of life or to make one an accepted member of society, today's mainstream society (MANE-stream seh-SIE-eh-tee) does not accept much beyond pierced ears. Most school principals and many employers agree that the status, or position in the community, of a person seeking an education or a job is not any better if his or her nose, lips, or eyebrows are pierced and glitter with jewelry. It is sometimes quite the opposite.

Why then has body piercing become so popular? Some people believe that jewelry in their ears, nose, lips, or eyebrows makes them more attractive. For many young people, it is fun to wear jewelry in unusual places. Celebrities and the world of fashion have set a trend, and young people often follow a fad, whether or not it is an accepted one.

Sometimes piercings are done to show membership in a counterculture (COWN-ter-cul-tyer) or special group, just as in some folk cultures in other places and times. Piercing can be a form of rebellion against mainstream society, like some tattoos. Piercings sometimes annoy parents, grandparents, and some

older people and that can encourage some young people to do it just to show that their age group is not the same as their parents'.

Could this be the fashion trend in the near future?

www.punchstock.com

In today's society we do not look quite as harshly at the practice of piercing as it did just a few decades ago. While many schools still have a strict ban on piercings, some have relaxed their rules just a bit and will allow a few kinds of piercings, such as in ears and noses, if the jewelry worn is small.

What is the future for bizarre body modification? When society reaches the point where tattoos and body piercings are no longer shocking, perhaps people who like to be daring will turn to surgical implants to change their appearance. Will horns be the next thing we see on foreheads as a fashion statement? Or perhaps the natural look will return and young people in fifty years will look back and laugh at the old timers for being so silly as to make holes in their bodies. Who knows? As one sociology professor said when commenting on all forms of body modification in both folk and modern societies: "They hurt, they bleed, and they last forever!"

Bibliography

Davis, Jinx. "Piercing: A Thread Through Time and Place." *Spectrum* - (2003).

Gengenbach, Heidi. "Boundaries of Beauty." *Journal of Women's History* - (Winter 2003).

Gray, Denis D. "Paudaung Giraffe Women." *Seattle Post Intelligencer.* Travel Section.

Leopold, Wendy. "First Person Stories of Chinese Foot Binding." *Northwestern News,* November 15, 1996.

"Living Canvas." *Newsweek* (1999).

Lloyd, J. D., ed. *Body Piercing and Tattoos.* San Diego, Calif.: Greenhaven - Press, 2003.

McNab, Nan. *Body Bizarre, Body Beautiful.* New York: Simon and Schuster, 2001.

Miller, Jean-Chris. *The Body Art Book: A Complete Illustrated Guide to Tattoos, Piercings, and Other Body Modifications.* New York: Berkley Books, 1997.

Pitts, Victoria. *In the Flesh: The Cultural Politics of Body Modification.* New - York: Palagrave Macmillan, 2003.

Powell, Charles A. *Bound Feet.* Boston: Warren Press, c. 1938.